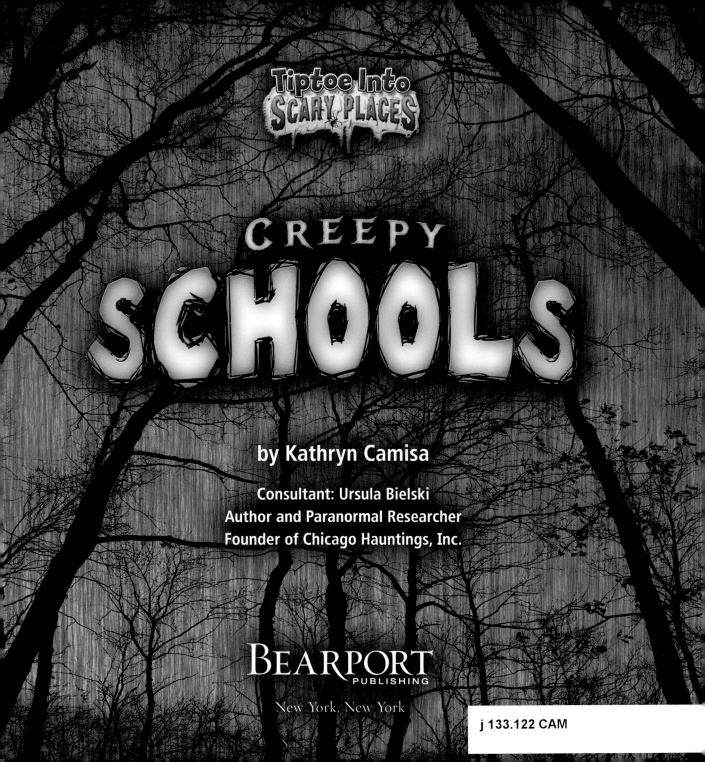

Tiptoe Into SCARY PLACES

CREEPY SCHOOLS

by Kathryn Camisa

Consultant: Ursula Bielski
Author and Paranormal Researcher
Founder of Chicago Hauntings, Inc.

BEARPORT
PUBLISHING

New York, New York

Credits

Cover, © Zacarias Pereira da Mata/Shutterstock, © Andrey Burmakin/Shutterstock, © Akova/Fotolia, and © Deyan Georgiev/Fotolia; TOC, © libertygal/iStock; 4–5, © jackjayDIGITAL/iStock, © Jakub Krechowicz/Shutterstock, and © Maria Arts/Shutterstock; 6, © Los Angeles Public Library Collection; 7, © Los Angeles Public Library Collection; 8, © elkor/iStock; 9, © Alex James Bramwell/Shutterstock, © Menna/Shutterstock, and © RAYBON/Shutterstock; 10–11, © COLOA Studio/Shutterstock; 10, © Thomas Hawk/CC BY-NC 4.0; 11, © Lario Tus/Shutterstock; 12, © Lario Tus/Shutterstock; 13, © GrahamMoore999/Shutterstock; 14, © 2017 Google; 15, © leisuretime70/Shutterstock; 16–17, © SvedOliver/Shutterstock and © kryzhov/Shutterstock; 18, © 2017 Google; 19, © Michael Courtney/Shutterstock and © George Marks/iStock; 20, © Olga Danylenko/Shutterstock; 21, © Tatyana Vyc/Shutterstock and © George Marks/iStock; 23, © Cheryl A. Meyer/Shutterstock; 24, © Paul Orr/Shutterstock.

Publisher: Kenn Goin
Editor: Jessica Rudolph
Creative Director: Spencer Brinker
Photo Researcher: Thomas Persano
Cover: Kim Jones

Library of Congress Cataloging-in-Publication Data in process at time of publication (2018)
Library of Congress Control Number: 2017005122
ISBN-13: 978-1-68402-272-4 (library binding)

For more information, write to Bearport Publishing Company, Inc., 45 West 21st Street, Suite 3B, New York, New York 10010. Printed in the United States of America.

10 9 8 7 6 5 4 3 2 1

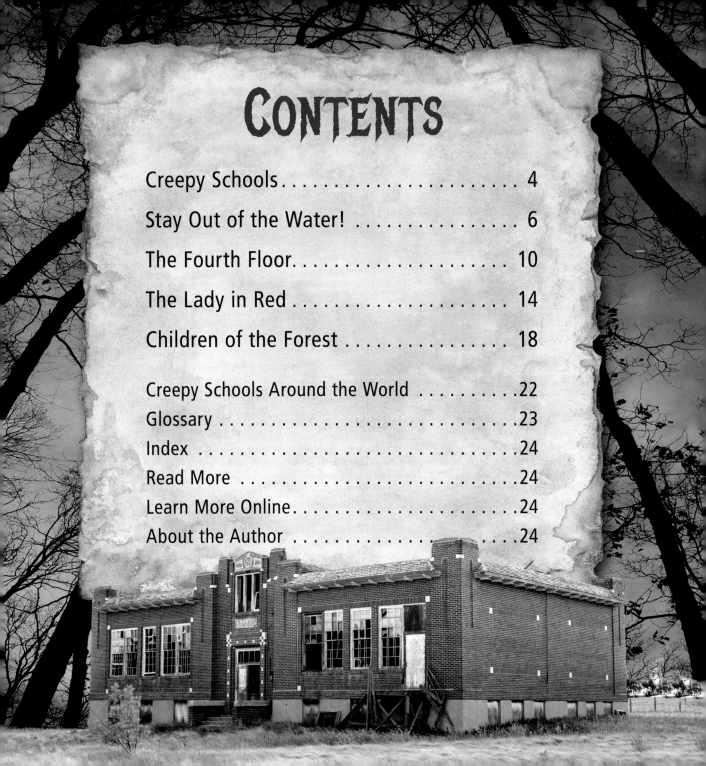

CONTENTS

CREEPY SCHOOLS

The bell has rung. Everyone has left the school building except you. You're almost to the exit when, suddenly, every locker door in the empty hallway swings wide open! *Creeeak.* As your heart pounds, you squeeze your eyes shut. Then you slowly open them. All the lockers are now closed! Was it only your imagination?

Get ready to read four chilling tales about creepy schools. Turn the page . . . if you have the nerve!

Stay Out of the Water!

Ramona Convent Secondary School, Alhambra, California

It was a warm fall morning in 1987. Students were about to arrive at school. Without warning, the ground started to rumble. The building swayed from side to side. **Debris** crashed to the ground.

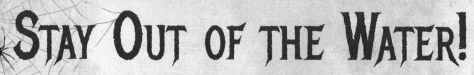

Damage to the school

6

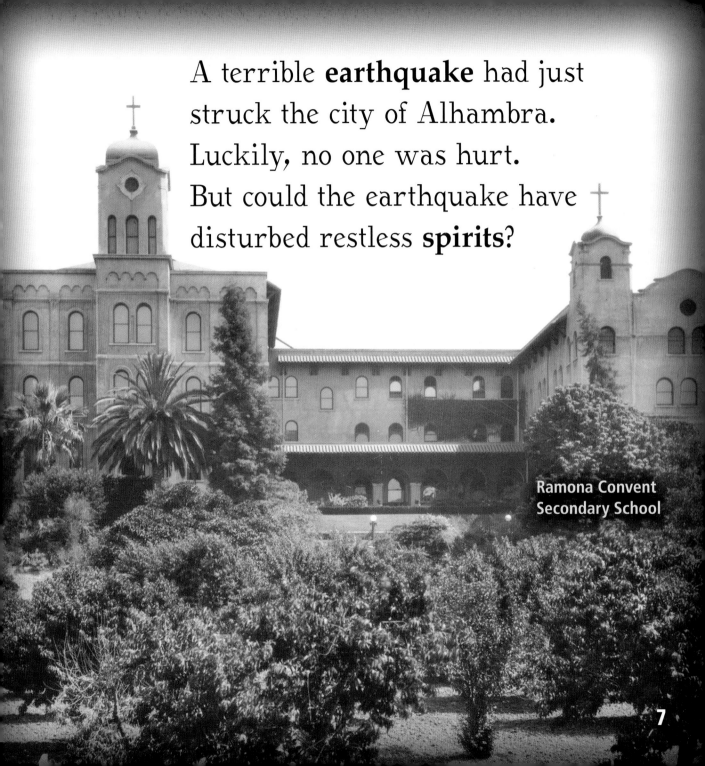

A terrible **earthquake** had just struck the city of Alhambra. Luckily, no one was hurt. But could the earthquake have disturbed restless **spirits**?

Ramona Convent Secondary School

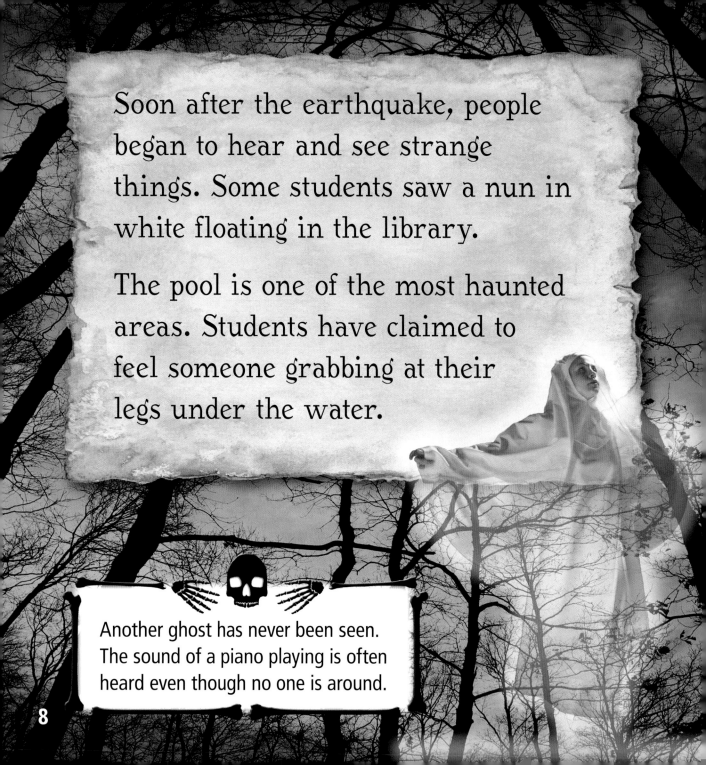

Soon after the earthquake, people began to hear and see strange things. Some students saw a nun in white floating in the library.

The pool is one of the most haunted areas. Students have claimed to feel someone grabbing at their legs under the water.

Another ghost has never been seen. The sound of a piano playing is often heard even though no one is around.

Many believe it's the ghost of a swimmer who drowned in the pool years ago. Some students are too scared to even go near the pool!

The Fourth Floor

El Paso High School, El Paso, Texas

Some areas of El Paso High School are closed to students and teachers. What could be **lurking** behind closed doors?

It's rumored that in the 1970s a girl jumped from the school's fourth-floor balcony and died. Ever since, many unusual events have occurred on the fourth floor.

El Paso High School

10

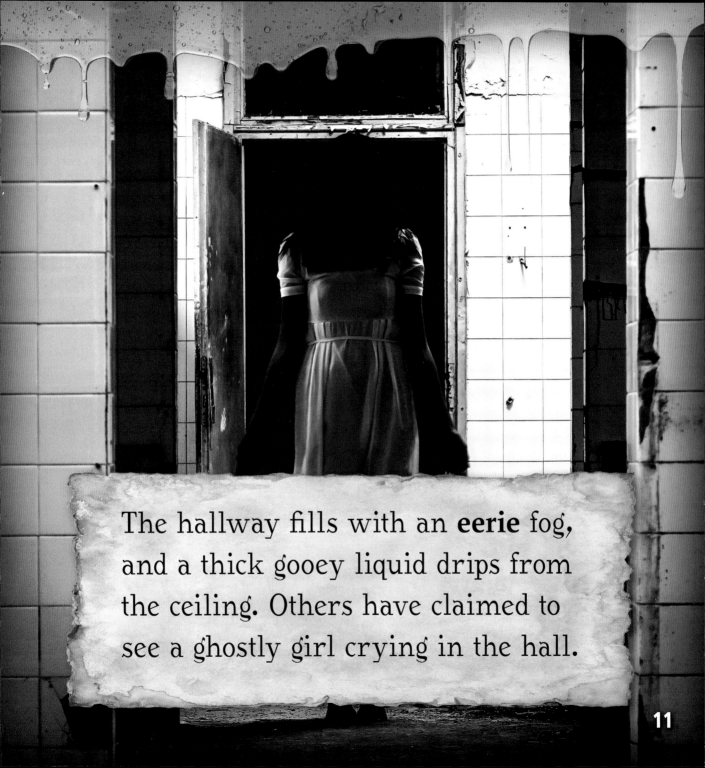

The hallway fills with an **eerie** fog, and a thick gooey liquid drips from the ceiling. Others have claimed to see a ghostly girl crying in the hall.

Another mystery haunts the school. In 1985, a photo was taken of the class. A blurry image of a student wearing all white appears in the center of the photo. Both teachers and students have said no one was standing in that spot when the photo was taken! Could the ghost of a former student be **lingering** at the school?

Today, the photo is displayed in a school trophy case. The identity of the ghostly figure remains unknown.

THE LADY IN RED

Tat Tak School, Hong Kong, China

The Tat Tak School closed in 1998. It's now nothing but gloomy **ruins.** Broken windows and discarded trash have **tarnished** the classrooms and grounds.

Several years ago, a group of teenagers explored the ruins.

Tat Tak School

First, they stopped by two tombstones on the property. That's when they heard the sound of footsteps. They looked around but didn't see anyone. Then, a girl in the group screamed!

Everyone turned and saw a ghostly lady in red floating nearby. The teenagers ran away in terror!

Many believe the teens had seen the **phantom** of a former school principal. She had hanged herself in the girls' bathroom. Her ghost is often seen wearing a red dress. Today, some people report seeing the spirit gazing out one of the school windows.

Local residents and taxi drivers refuse to drive near Tat Tak School for fear of meeting the ghost!

CHILDREN OF THE FOREST

Fallsvale Elementary School, Forest Falls, California

It's early morning. The sun peeks through the trees. A little girl wearing a bright pink shirt steps out of Fallsvale Elementary School. She sees something strange in the distance and stares.

A group of children are playing by a wooden fence. Their clothes appear old-fashioned and colorless. Suddenly, the children . . . disappear! Could mysterious ghosts be haunting the forest?

Fallsvale Elementary was built in 1935 near an **abandoned** school. There's a fence around the old building. But it seems the **barrier** can't prevent spirits inside the former school from wandering away.

Many claim the ghosts of schoolchildren haunt the abandoned building. There have been many reports of these spirits roaming, dancing, and playing in the forest.

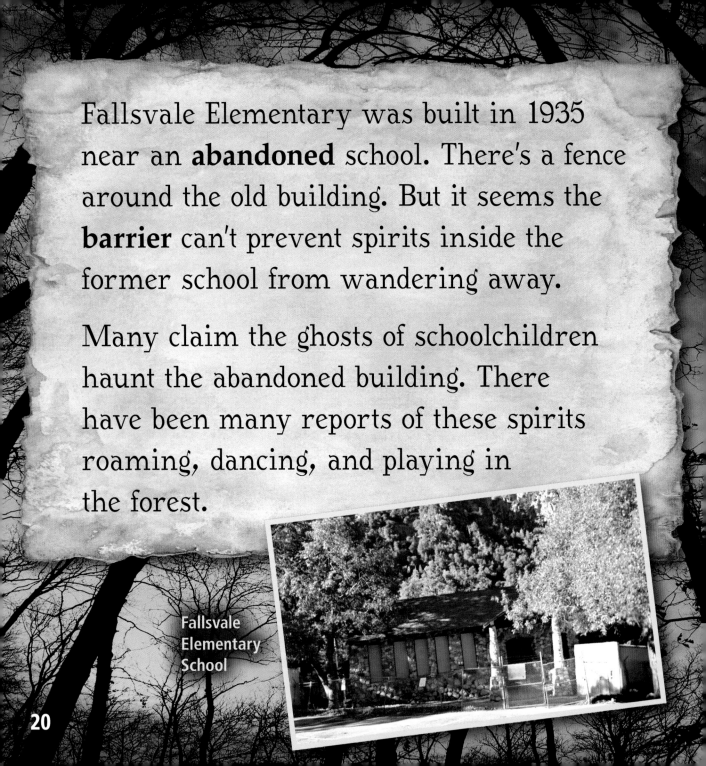

Fallsvale Elementary School

They are even known to interact with the living schoolchildren from Fallsvale Elementary!

The Fallsvale Elementary schoolchildren aren't afraid of their ghostly peers. In fact, many kids even know some of the ghosts by name!

CREEPY SCHOOLS
AROUND THE WORLD

RAMONA CONVENT SECONDARY SCHOOL
Alhambra, California

Discover a school that is home to restless spirits.

FALLSVALE ELEMENTARY SCHOOL
Forest Falls, California

Visit a school haunted by ghost children!

EL PASO HIGH SCHOOL
El Paso, Texas

Explore one of the most haunted schools in Texas.

TAT TAK SCHOOL
Hong Kong, China

Check out an abandoned school where a lady in red still lingers.

NORTH AMERICA

EUROPE

ASIA

Atlantic Ocean

AFRICA

Pacific Ocean

Pacific Ocean

SOUTH AMERICA

Indian Ocean

AUSTRALIA

Atlantic Ocean

Southern Ocean

ANTARCTICA

Glossary

abandoned (uh-BAN-duhnd) left empty and uncared for

barrier (BA-ree-ur) something that blocks the way

debris (duh-BREE) the remains of something that has been destroyed

earthquake (URTH-kwayk) a shaking of the ground caused by the sudden movement of rocks below Earth's surface

eerie (IHR-ee) mysterious, strange

lingering (LING-gur-ing) staying in a place longer than is usual or expected

lurking (LURK-ing) secretly hiding

phantom (FAN-tuhm) a ghost

ruins (ROO-inz) the remains of something that has been destroyed

spirits (SPIHR-its) supernatural beings such as ghosts

tarnished (TAR-nishd) spoiled by decay or neglect

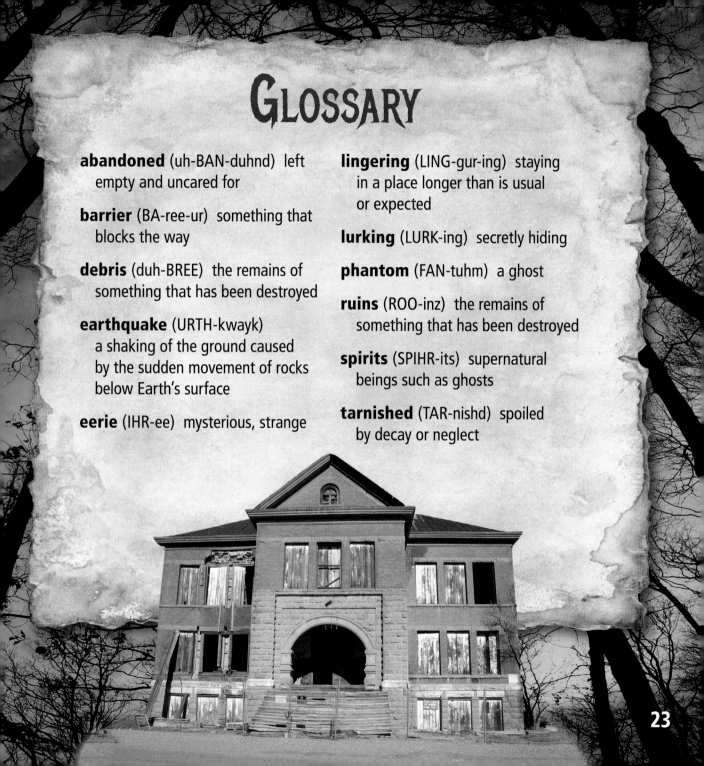

INDEX

READ MORE

Phillips, Dee. *The Ghostly Secret of Lakeside School (Cold Whispers II).* New York: Bearport (2017).

San Souci, Robert D. *A Terrifying Taste of Short & Shivery: Thirty Creepy Tales.* New York: Random House (2011).

LEARN MORE ONLINE

To learn more about creepy schools, visit:
www.bearportpublishing.com/Tiptoe

ABOUT THE AUTHOR

Kathryn Camisa is an author who once stayed at a castle that some believe to be haunted. Unfortunately, she did not meet any ghosts during her visit.